Six Sundays Toward a Seventh

The Poiema Poetry Series

Poems are windows into worlds; windows into beauty, goodness, and truth; windows into understandings that won't twist themselves into tidy dogmatic statements; windows into experiences. We can do more than merely peer into such windows; with a little effort we can fling open the casements, and leap over the sills into the heart of these worlds. We are also led into familiar places of hurt, confusion, and disappointment, but we arrive in the poet's company. Poetry is a partnership between poet and reader, seeking together to gain something of value—to get at something important.

Ephesians 2:10 says, "We are God's workmanship . . ." *poiema* in Greek —the thing that has been made, the masterpiece, the poem. The Poiema Poetry Series presents the work of gifted poets who take Christian faith seriously, and demonstrate in whose image we have been made through their creativity and craftsmanship.

These poets are recent participants in the ancient tradition of David, Asaph, Isaiah, and John the Revelator. The thread can be followed through the centuries—through the diverse poetic visions of Dante, Bernard of Clairvaux, Donne, Herbert, Milton, Hopkins, Eliot, R.S. Thomas, and Denise Levertov—down to the poet whose work is in your hand. With the selection of this volume you are entering this enduring tradition, and as a reader contributing to it.

—D. S. Martin
  Series Editor

Six Sundays Toward a Seventh

Spiritual Poems by Sydney Lea

(21 February—3 April, 1988)

CASCADE *Books* · Eugene, Oregon

SIX SUNDAYS TOWARDS A SEVENTH
Spiritual Poems by Sydney Lea

Copyright © 2012 Sydney Lea. All rights reserved. Except for brief quotations in critical publications or reviews, no part of this book may be reproduced in any manner without prior written permission from the publisher. Write: Permissions, Wipf and Stock Publishers, 199 W. 8th Ave., Suite 3, Eugene, OR 97401.

Cascade Books
An Imprint of Wipf and Stock Publishers
199 W. 8th Ave., Suite 3
Eugene, OR 97401

www.wipfandstock.com

ISBN 13: 978-1-61097-681-7

Cataloging-in-Publication data

Lea, Sydney, 1942–

    Six sundays toward a seventh : spiritual poems by sydney lea / Sydney Lea.

    The Poiema Poetry Series.

    x + 96 p., 23 cm.

    ISBN: 978-1-61097-681-7

PS 3562 E16 S5 2012

Manufactured in the U.S.A.

For the fellowship of
The First Congregational Church
of Newbury, Vermont

If during meditation our thoughts move to persons who are near to us or to those we are concerned about, then let them linger there.

—Dietrich Bonhoeffer, Meditating On the Word

Contents

Acknowledgments | ix

I. Doubt, Despond, Defiance | 1

Incantation against Revelation | 2
Sin and Fear (1957) | 5
Doubt | 7
Making Sense | 10
Late Season | 13
It Has Orange Teeth | 15
Small Jeremiad | 17

II. Midway | 19

Recalling the Horseman Billy Farrell
 from an Airplane in Vermont | 20
No Sign | 22
Pietà | 26
Prayer for the Little City | 29
Leonora's Kitchen | 31
Midway | 33
Manifest | 36
The Floating Candles | 38
In the Blind | 41
Pianissimo | 44
The Return | 46
Road Agent | 50
Over Brogno | 54

III. Wonder | 59

For Faith | 60
Ghost Pain | 62
Hole | 65
At a Solemn Musick | 68
Wonder: Red Beans and Ricely | 70
Barnet Hill Brook | 73
Dispute with Thomas Hardy | 75
Transport | 77
Sober | 79

IV. Six Sundays Toward a Seventh | 81

Acknowledgments

The New Yorker, Leonora's Kitchen, The Return: Intensive Care, The Floating Candles

The Christian Century, Hole, Transport, Barnet Hill Brook, Dispute with Thomas Hardy

Iron Horse, Pursuit of a Wound

The Atlantic, Midway, Children Singing

Salmagundi, Small Jeremiad

New England Review, Doubt

Poetry, Over Brogno

The Missouri Review, In the Blind

The New Republic, Making Sense

Prairie Schooner, Late Season, Pietà

The American Scholar, It Has Orange Teeth

Hudson Review, Recalling the Horseman Billy Farrell from an Airplane in Vermont

Crazyhorse, No Sign

The Partisan Review, Manifest

Grand Street, Pianissimo

Antaeus, For Faith

The Georgia Review, Sober

Image, Ghost Pain

The Southern Review, Wonder: Red Beans and Ricely

The Kenyon Review, Six Sundays Toward a Seventh

Most of these poems also appeared in prior volumes, as follows:

Searching the Drowned Man: Incantation Against Revelation, Recalling the Horseman Billy Farrell from an Airplane in Vermont

The Floating Candles: Sin and Fear, The Floating Candles

No Sign: Making Sense, Midway, The Return: Intensive Care, Leonora's Kitchen, No Sign, Pietà

The Blainville Testament: Road Agent, In the Blind

Prayer for the Little City: Over Brogno, Late Season, For Faith, Six Sundays Toward a Seventh, Prayer for the Little City, Manifest

Pursuit of a Wound: It Has Orange Teeth, Pursuit of a Wound

Ghost Pain: Hole, Ghost Pain, At a Solemn Musick, Wonder: Red Beans and Ricely, Transport

Young of the Year: Dispute with Thomas Hardy

I. Doubt, Despond, Defiance

Incantation against Revelation

> *On that day there shall be neither cold nor frost. And there shall be continuous day (it is known to the Lord), not day and not night, for at evening time there shall be light.*
>
> —Zechariah 14:6

Let it not be.
Let winter-clipped day
rush to dark
and insufficient clarity
of partial light from impartial moons.
All day,
let snow drift over
famished vision,
slat fences be buried
like bones in our meat
or an instinct, hidden
in harmless
indecipherable charades of sleep.
In darkness.
Let Lord not be one Lord, not be
Lord of One.

Let the country have night
in which beasts
predictably fool us
with their footfalls, cries
spilling from mazy
buckbrush, trees.
None like another.
Let the country be

full of animal rites:
the whip-poor-will"'s click and hum in praise
of his mate, the fox's
imperfect circle
round his bed before bedding.
Woodcock tumble
through skies of April.
All day, a mystery of bees.

Let prophecy of the day the fall
foliage will turn
remain inept,
and stately tamaracks
turn to ferns,
their cascades of yellow needles a sign,
and nothing to signify.
Let cold and frost descend
to freeze the slap
of a million waves
in difficult runes over hosts of fry
of cloudiest fate. Let people not cry
the one tear designed
to end tears.
Let many a woman and man
for the cloudiest reasons be brave.

And let there be years,
seasons, the colorful comings
and goings of grief,
bolting flowers, exquisite
unmeaning in all
our protests at darkness,
pleas for relief.

Incantation against Revelation

Let an ending to number
be unimaginable:
butterflies
—vulnerable Monarchs—dismay
with their profligate stratagems,
wind-battered waste-motion miles;
in suicide
barnacles cluster
like salt clots over the piles

of docks, as many as seeds
of mustard, in harbors of cities
bigger than Zion
where the harsh bouquet of sulfur
clouds and softens
the looming high-rises like pity
so that out of discomfort
rises high splendor
and nowhere is pure
white Light

nor reduction in mind's quantity. . . .
Let us suffer. . . .
Let us hail
the intimate hum of insects, say,
returning by thousands at night
and say

at least at last, There is
this order prevails.

Sin and Fear (1957)

A slate-color heron stood as the ground fog cleared and changed
to soup of August. No motion. Even the salamanders
the heron stabbed each morning settled into mud
so still the great bird's pondering eye could not detect them.
That wicked eye appeared—impossibly—to droop.
The ducks of Swamp Creek, moulting now, began to hop
frog-awkward, flightless, out of wilted pickerelweed.
We crouched in a blind on shore.
We were all but naked, dressed in swimming trunks to be
our own retrievers. Just beyond point-blank,
we'd blow the grainy mallards' heads off, pluck and cook them
in the evening cool. We waited for the ducks to school
so as to slaughter more than one with every shot,
and huddled in that quick-breathed wait as close as lovers.
A lifeless breeze cuffed at the pond, the cattail and weed.
We saw it riffle dingy feathers. But it carried, too,
somehow a smell of suppurating carcass, harsh
and dreary all at once. It seemed at least to me
the stench the soul must make in wrenching free
of the body, to flap along the suffocating lonely
ages into the Hell they talked about on Sunday.
Uphill behind us
out of sight, there was the sound of labored breathing,
or was it wings? Across the swamps and fields just then
there came the awful howling of my uncle's hunting dogs,
unlikely energetic in such a torpid dawn,
and way off in the shimmering pasture horses reared
and whinnied, bolting headlong in spite of summer bellies.
The ducks left the brook a lather, kicking for absolute center

of the gray-brown slough. Then all was quiet again.
We skulked in terror homeward, Charlie, Michael, I—
two dead now, fifty years gone by. I can't explain
that fear, the way our tears sprang up! Then dried.

Doubt

Something wakes me in the west of Montana.
Mouse in the hallway? Wind down the mesa?

Rented room, moonshine sinister.
I feel old, I have to tend my bladder,

And so I swing my feet to the floor,
Swing them, awkward, to the ice-smooth floor.

It's not its bareness, its vivid void,
That jolts me cold in the stark frank light

But a phrase that comes: *A patch of bare floor. . . .*
That clutch of words: it somehow appalls.

I shudder and settle back in the clothes
Till I think other words, too grandiose—

Eli, Eli, lama sabachthani?—
But it's January here in my body.

Not only from loneliness. Shame as well
That the light of a life can so quickly be quelled

By the darkness behind this other light.
It's thousands of miles from toilet to cot.

I've come out here to try the fishing.
I can't seem to care if I ever go fishing,

Or do much again of anything.
The world's on the cusp of vanishing

When I suddenly have odd company:
I think of John, back in the country

Of verdant Vermont, of his brother who beat
Their likeable father all but dead

Then shot himself, the Oxy-Contin
Scorching his veins—or what was left of them.

John's wife was our storekeeper's youngest daughter.
She ran away with some newcomer lawyer

And now John restores old cars "instead
Of talking too much with the Man in My Head.

"Ten minutes of that and I'll make myself sick,"
Or so he tells me. To whom will *I* talk?

I have no skills, not a lonely one.
Better to foul myself where I've lain,

To stay in bed under fetid blankets.
That open floor: I don't dare chance it.

Better to gibber "Old Mother Hubbard"
Or mouth this scrap of blues I conjure

*—Sugar for sugar, salt for salt.
If you don't love me it ain't my fault—*

Than keep talking to no one, no one myself,
Or still worse, to my own Man in the Head.

Better to loll in self-pity, Lord,
Than step across that bare patch of floor.

—*Holter Lake, Montana, September 2004*

Making Sense

A tatting of wings this morning
broke silence, and dream:
a spider tethered a wasp to a mullion.
I tried, failing,
to resist my own translation—
Just as the field growth arrays
itself in summer seed-fringe, it seems,
each thing in its way
begins to prepare
for winter, inside and out.
The kingdoms below us all season
have eaten and given
themselves to be eaten without
remark or record, have known fears
and lusts but not
as a man might know them:
as nooses
mounted the wings in a silken
skein, to spider and wasp,
there occurred
perhaps some version
of *Here is an end
of all this.*
Don't call it neurosis.
Their vibrations
were routine,
professional, unlike those
of a man,

one who sees how the knuckles of one hand
have turned to white onions,
and picks at his food, and
looks out the windows
through the light
spare rain.
He is inside.
Try to project
him seated there as the panes
begin with the night
to close off the pond, barn, corn piece, the last few
nighthawks slicing the last few
ephemerids from air.
As the glass collects
the dark and dew
and reflects
his small sequestered dwelling's contents
back upon him, like conscience,
or simple consciousness,
try to picture him there.
Try to imagine him try
to make nothing
of all this, to make sense
of his day, his situation,
by making outward sense
an alternative to meditation:
sight, the great turtle
he confronted when, at dawn, he pried
the hatch of his well,
and deeper in, the gutted carp in the pool;
by noon, he could *smell*
wine in the wind off windfall apples
where late-laid larvae will die;
touch, in late afternoon,
when the lame hand brushed a spit bug's drool;

the bug's unlikely whistle
will do for *sound*,
heard before supper; for *taste*,
his recall
now of an odd flavor like charcoal
in the scarred skin over his late wife's
late left breast.
For all of which the word is *Trouble*,
trouble, trouble! Not a growth from
the ground, but the ground itself
of self, which will not leave
all this alone.

I want the old man's grief
to be the winter-silent pain
of the body alone.
I want the old man older than I
to lend authority.
I want him to have learned by the end
of all this to make sense
no more than sense.
But see the hand
tense, like something that wants to take flight.
The spider has long since
retreated into sleep,
the wasp hanging
drugged in his casing.
Without comment.
Forever quiet.
But listen.
The old man will speak.
He is inside.
He will go on speaking,
I fear, into the night.

Late Season

This was the last I'd trouble the ducks this season:
there'd be skim-ice on the sloughs
and later, snow come down from Canada, horizontal.
There might be some luck, a little . . .
no, more. It was already there, beforehand:
dirt road near dawn, canoe
snubbed in the pickup's bed,

and in my lap the great good head
of my dog, the blood in his graying muzzle
a pulse in my leg as we bucked the ruts.
And, come down from a Canada even farther,
music, local notices, news of the weather—
the radio's early report. I imagined the struggle
of a farmer there. Up like me. *Good mutt,* I whispered. I scratched

the retriever's neck.
It was warm. Reception good. The farmer leaned
in mind into winds that they say
can straighten a tow-chain out behind a tractor.
I liked driving tractor-slow, imagining that weather.
Plenty of time. Down here, whatever the wind,
I could count for now on a milder day.
I was forty-five. I liked how the a.m. signal

said something about what it was to be fuddled,
or rather how static fell away when your object was clear:
getting from house to barn and back in a gale;
getting the decoys out before you froze;

getting into the proper kinds of clothes
to meet a day. Getting it right. A cold time of year,
but for now I was snug behind the wheel,
and already I could envision

the redleg black duck blown down and past in migration,
the reach of a wave from the farther shore of the river
toward me, where I'd sit, alone but for the dog.
Wave like a single important announcement.
A blind of fragile reeds, and all around it
the signs of how we must seek to save forever
what we receive of what goes by: a buck
who has left his ghostly track in slush and mud;

gleam of low sun in old blood;
spent shells, drifting clumps of insubstantial feather,
gone in a moment, abiding in the mind;
feel of a dog companion's eager breathing
turned to frost on your cheek, then melting to nothing.
Later the awful snow would come to the river,
and later the careful blind no longer stand,

nor dog, nor duck, nor I, nor Canada farmer.

It Has Orange Teeth

—*after a story told me by the late L. C.*

He made it a habit to cast his *dorothea*
—each night, all that June long—to one trophy trout,
whose skepticism cured Lesley of being a dreamer
for the moment; that was what fishing a fly was about,

he told me: the world come down to pure concentration.
You saw the rise, you threw a line above it,
no further thought entered—not self, not family, not nation.
You were both away and clearheaded. That's why he loved it,

Remotely, like loving your way through a tumble of water,
mindful only of boulders and eddies, the rest,
the universe, having shrunk. There was only disaster
if he let his mind or canoe go anywhere else.

He said that he timed false casts to his quick breath's rhythm,
then dropped the dun on the slick, while overhead bats
and swallows were hunting, although he didn't see them.
(Everything superficial, I punned.)
The slap

behind him felt something, therefore, akin to the blow
a sheriff once fetched him. The cop suspected narcosis,
not his first grand mal. What oddly had seemed like a flow
in his life—a current bound to draw him the closest

he'd ever get to a kind of blessed distraction—
turned into a mangle of strobe light, obscenity, threat.
That night it was only a beaver, whose own concentration
lay in getting her way to the west, to her twig-hungry kits.

Bank beavers, he said, whose home "weren't no more than a hole
in the high-rolling tier by the rapids," which Lesley at last
was compelled to notice. Cliché came to serve him: "My soul,"
he said, "was all nightmares: present, future, and past,

"and each ran into the other, and each of them nameless."
The beaver's a creature so placid you might call her staid.
In fable, she represents the virtue of habits,
but her warning caused Lesley to hear rebukes from the dead

for spending his time in trying to obliterate time;
he'd spent too much at conniving to get himself laid
or at trout or at poker, nights when he should have been home:
too much in indifference, his wife lying cancerous in bed.

Les reeled, then stuck his fly in the rod grip's cork.
The beaver pounded again, then glided cross-river.
Dizzy, he feared a seizure there in the dark
for the first time in years. Had he taken the pills? He shivered.

After that evening, he never again went out wading.
It seemed hard enough to get through a day on dry land.
He never made out what the river ghosts had been saying.
Yet they had addressed him, he knew. And a terror remained.

Small Jeremiad

I killed a catbird once when I was young.
I'll claim to this day I didn't really mean to,
Just noticed him and flung a thoughtless stone.

I've done much worse, so why would this live on?
My cracked LP is *Mulligan Meets Getz.*
I killed a catbird once when I was young

but why, awake at daylight, should I have turned
from husky saxes chanting "That Old Feeling"
to some poor bird at whom I flung a stone?

There seems reason enough: a catbird dropped to our lawn
As I chose my old-fashioned record, a rare bird here
in northern New England, and though I've cast no stone,

I'm sunk in lamentation. Things I have done.
Ones I have left undone. And that old feeling. . . .
I killed a catbird once when I was young.

My life's the only life I'll ever own.
I own it all when memory flies in.
I killed a catbird once when I was young.
I noticed him and flung a thoughtless stone.

II. Midway

Recalling the Horseman Billy Farrell from an Airplane in Vermont

—in mem. Robert Penn Warren and Eleanor Clark

He watched a cloud. It brought him
the shape of one horse or another:
"Was it Cinders? I disremember . . .
a big trot . . . early autumn,
grass to the pommel. September."

Toward dark the ridges smothered
day. The rattling wagon
winnowed birds. How smart
his bays—"like hens on hot stone"—
that drew us along. I've discovered

the painter's failure of heart.
I've tried to draw his face
from the land, his language, the land
in his language: "Damn the wind!
Enough to shake owls from the trees!"

They come back, every phrase;
but I've lost his face in the clouds.
You learn in time to fail.
He spat on the hardening road,
bad heel propped on the rail,

as out of the grain fields the geese
flew, the time flew, September

Recalling the Horseman Billy Farrell from an Airplane in Vermont

he darkened and died.
Heart rattles. Strange as disease
or god, the airplane roars

down the ridges. Wind shakes. Auroras
rise and whack at the sky.
Frost on the tarmac glints
and goes out like sparks off hooves,
or the face I can't remember,

but off to the west I squint
at a spot out of actual sight,
and Billy mounts and moves.

No Sign

What can we learn from Calvin,
a god-fearing man
by his own description, but also a little insane,
as he liked to say?

You'd call him simple.
But aren't we all inclined
to believe that life revolves on radical signs?

He bought a turquoise camper,
for instance, because she was growing away—his daughter
Debbie, sixteen;
and Jimmie, eleven, was showing
hints of the adolescent estrangement coming:
the feint of a sneer,
the brows that ground together,
feet that shuffled. Now, thought Calvin, or never.

Something to hold us
at least for a while together.
The longer Calvin looked, the brighter it seemed,
the rig with its chromium trim,
its velveteen carpet,
its logo (a leaping fish)—
until at last it became incarnate Wish,
a lust at once betokened and satisfied
without a trace of guilt,
like the craving for grace
that might yet in his life be realized. . . .

Ninety a month,
after two hundred down.

His wife pretended to fume
when he drove it home,
pointing wordless to the chipped weather side
of their bungalow,
to the dent in the gravel drive
that swelled with mud. But she was the same old Lizzy
at last, and giggled.
"1 know," said Cal. "I'm crazy."

The Bingo had started again at the church in May,
when they didn't need oil or wood
to heat the vestry.
The men slapped Cal on the back and shook their heads.
The women applauded
the camper's color; one said,
"like Mary's robe." Everyone laughed. One night,
Calvin and Red
and Woody took a ride
with their beers along the country roads. They all
got sentimental,
imagined a lake in fall
way up north at sunset on Calvin's behalf:
trout on the surface;
through an oxbow, the last
pillars of sun on the water; the wild loons' cackle.
"1 can smell the fried fish as they sizzle,"
said Red, and friendly Woody—crude as ever—
imagined the family
"happy as hogs in manure."

Cal dropped them off and drove himself home on air.

No Sign

You can't help wishing
the whole thing ended there.
It seems almost unnecessary to say
that things did not shape up exactly that way:
Debbie's a logger's mistress;
Jimmie, the boy,
is a dynamite cap of trouble.

Perhaps we should skip the intrigue,
and should keep from saying that Calvin was nuts to believe
that he could ever carry out his purpose
—bringing the family together—
with something so rootless.
For the Lord knows Calvin was rough enough on himself.
He took the camper's corrosions
as moral rebuff.
Heaven was now and forever hopeless, beyond him.
You wouldn't think
he could be so damned despondent.
Everything signaled shame: that dirty gaping
ravine in the mud,
the scars on his house's clapboard.
Calvin resorted to weeping
when he looked at Lizzy,

her hair and features fading,
the stay-at-home appearance of her clothing.

Until at last
one morning the pastor selected
these words from the Gospel of Mark for his sermon's text:
"Why does this generation seek a sign?"
Whether or not
the preacher had Calvin in mind,
Calvin heard it that way.

He thought of Debbie:
what bonded him
together with her? with Jimmie?

"Truly I say to you no sign will be given"
—the Gospel quoted Jesus—"to this generation."

If there's a lesson here,
perhaps it's one
that occurred to Calvin then. It came to him
not like Revelation,
a flash of force,
but plain and simple: things will take their course.

Pietà

—in mem. M.K. Lea (1944–1980)

It is not any single version
that moves me so, but all: great Buonarotti's
no more than the one I bought as if to mock it
on its smarmy Venetian postcard whose cake-pink Virgin's

tears bring me tears. That He is grown
(as much an adult, you could say, as she)
is part of what weighs on me.
But who's it for, this grief of mine,

this mourning? The fact of touch. And the mystery—
sublime or vulgar, sobbing or stoic,
the two are ever other. Crude, heroic,
distracted, whatever. In every rendering I see,

so other. Of course there's sadness that a mother
should posture with her blasted seed, but fineness,
surely, too. I wonder if Kliney,
my oddly named and fated brother,

before the hemorrhage fully blacked his brain,
felt some such mother-touch.
Once he'd left the breast, there wasn't much
by way of laying-on of hands

between those two. This poem
assigns no blame to either party. I

am the one who writes it, I who've shied
as much as he from home,

as much beyond her reach.
Or no, not quite as much. I'm still alive.
I don't know how I've reached this dim surmise
that as the pale tube leached

its useless glucose nurture from a sack
and the EEG's thin scribble flattened out
she dropped the bright steel rail and put
her fingers to his face—but that

is the thing that touches me beyond all reason.
That, and the counter-vision, that as in life,
in death as well the two were stiff
and formal, blood between them

too much, and years, and that the Anglo-
Saxon sequesters passion out of sight.
Does everyone sometimes? That night,
dazed farmers, as they angled

headstrong herds to fold, may well have mumbled
clichés on weather, games and levies,
like us when things, as the saying goes, get heavy.
And heavy they'd been. Earliest miracle

in fact was maybe that Mary was enlightened
—in every sense the word can carry—
enough to hold him there, to parry
the nuisance thrusts of insects, cleanse him, frighten

away the innocent rubbernecking kids.
Miracle of grace—or was it courage?

Pietà

The funeral lacked all cant or flourish.
You sat erect there, Mother. What you did

three days before in the darkened ward
I've never learned. This is a kind of guessing,
maybe a way of asking.
To hold a ruined man who's yours

as husband, friend or lover
can never be. . . .
It is the unthinkable notion that touches me,
as much your flesh as the ruined brother.

The notion and the posture, and he within it,
manchild, or maybe not at all.
As I might be. Pity. Pietá.
Mercy. I could think to want it.

Prayer for the Little City

—January 6, 1995

Hushed plane, the pond. Ice-fishers' lights. Still little city.
Men hug their whiskey jugs inside as they loiter among
whiffs of bait, potbelly smoke, sock-wool and sweat.

Laconic chat: an idle joke; or God damn that
or God damn this, although such words aren't even angry,
but ordinary. Snowmobile roads thread our shacks

one to another; now and then, Big Lou throws open
his door (like an oven's, infernal within) and cries to a neighbor,
"Doin' some good?" Or dirty Duane, the one we call

"Blackfly," will call words much the same and the neighborhood
will rally from silence a moment or two, then sink back in.
It's half past ten. Blackfly and Lou and all the quietened

others stay through the darkness till dawn, whether or not
the small smelt bite. What of this town, this bob-house crew?
What of Ben, who's outside skimming his ice-hole's *o*'s?

He sniffs and blows, thinks vaguely of women, and thinks to name
some part of their bodies out loud across the frozen surface:
a shout all worthless, directionless, a shout all shoddy

with platitude, devoid of embrace, containing nothing,
not even longing . . . at least for sex. Just part of a mood
and situation much at odds, it might be imagined,

Prayer for the Little City

with a hopeful season, season of gods, of resolution
to start anew. Outside, the flags on their planted poles
in the utter chill are utterly slack, betraying no

visionary prey down under to clasp our lures.
The dullness is pure. No signs, no wonders, no mystery . . .
except it be the care with which all night men linger,

as if in prayer for a novel fish, or a novel way
by which to address some thing they're feeling. Surely this is
part of what holds us under crude ceilings beaded with pitch,

amid this fetor with speechless friends. Surely, surely
a sense that early, before the dawn (or sooner, or later)
our flags will all at once, together, tremble and shimmy.

Epiphany —o bright palaver! o every hole
a yodel of steam! So runs our fancy in the absence of sound
in this merest of towns, although our shanties' very beams

of light seem bored. O little city, we think, it's cold;
city, how still, how still we see thee. Still, the stars
go by above, even here, and still may love

embrace the year.

Leonora's Kitchen

Imagine we do not know that she was so young,
that she encountered a sudden illness and fell,
gone out to the hencoop to gather eggs
for Sunday night's light supper.
The men and her boys are in town.
In the simple kitchen, the radio stutters with lightning
that flashes far off, near the station.
On the table in the middle of the room
stands a colander of beans,
red tomatoes that sweat on the oilcloth's design,
the cloth translucent
in every crease, it has been there so long.

The light is peculiar,
as if some realist painter had found a method
with light that holds the painting's mystery.
The scene can't yet be informed
by any particular pathos—
we haven't learned she lies out there,
the white hens walking idly near her,
stepping now and then across her ankles.
We cannot yet be moved to picture
one of them perched for a time on the swell of her hip,
cocking its head, spreading its meager
feckless wings and jumping down.

And the kitchen itself: it seems to do nothing
but replicate the kitchen in any house
of the country working poor,

framed as it is by porch pillars, bowed,
a floor bowed up,
a ceiling down.

The light is the apparent light of southern
Illinois on any of fifty or sixty
humid evenings, from far away
the flashes of heat.
Soon the moths will tattoo the screens,
beige on rust. She hasn't been discovered,
so the fact that she was young, was pretty and decent,
cannot mean anything yet,
if in fact it will ever mean anything.
We can't imagine in this moment
the room illuminated by anything

like that aura said to rise off the spirit rising.
Yet somehow, still, it is radiant,
and moves us, though unmoving.

Midway

> ... *He asked him, "Do you see anything?" And he looked up and said, "I see men; but they look like trees, walking." Then again he laid hands upon his eyes; and he looked intently, and was restored, and saw everything clearly.*
>
> —Mark 8:23-25

January.
The hours after midday are coming
back, there is time
to climb from home
to height of land for the broader vision:
north and east,
Mount Moosilauke,
its four rivers of snow conjoining;
directly west,
the little town
on the highway, all its citizens
without a doubt
preoccupied
with matters they find as grave as any;
and all around,

the traffic of beasts,
invisible now, great and tiny.
A pregnant jumble,
near and far,
then and now, in a time of year
stormy and frigid,
but I have sweated,
stripped to the waist, it has been so clear.

The dead have been dead
it seems so long,

and yet their ghosts are perched on every
branch above me,
cloaking themselves
in the rising vapors from my body,
the day's sole clouds.

Deep in the Sunday
village, forlorn, the sound of swings
in the empty schoolyard
clinking against
their cold steel standards, like diminished
steeple bells:
ten o'clock's
sparse service was over hours
ago. My father
lays hands on my sight
up here, and friends, and my furious brother,
who at last seems calm.
The night is losing
its sovereignty, it will not be
overlong

before it loses
its winter boast, "Come out with me,
come out and stay,
and you'll be a corpse."
The crickets, partridge, frogs will all
come back to drum
their victory;
the whippoorwills will make their hum
and click as they mate,
the freshets will loosen;

the children, done for the year with lessons,
will elect to throng
the grassy playground. . . .
The past will turn itself over, shaking
out my brother,

friends, and father,
and they will be as before, but better,
as I will be,
unless—as so often—
I'm dreaming here; unless what I sense
is just another
misty version
of lifelong longing. It's hard to say. . . .
A moment ago,
I flushed a crowd
of flying squirrels, who in their soaring
out of their holes
looked so like angels
I rubbed my eyes. And what do I see?
On the far horizon
appears to be
a line of men, there in procession . . .
as darkness deepens, they look like trees.

Manifest

—litany: winter walk

In evergreens, wind-riven,
        whose blaze-orange wounds
        at limb and crown certify passion;
in the mitten-wool taste
        of snow you scoop to your mouth
        because—so you imagine—you thirst;
in illogical woodpeckers' laughter,
        in their swooping flight,
        that suggests assertion crossed by doubt;
in rough-frozen rims of tracks
        the animals left in the dark preceding
        nights, whose meaning needs no glozing;
in the hue of a beech
        —neither quite somber gray
        nor placid blue—that teases all sight and belief;
in the way this sun at solstice
        jumps up from the hill
        and asks no reading, but affirmation in the chill;
in the ermine who fought the owl,
        resisting negation:
        alone now, scarlet in snow—conspicuous, stiffened;
in the steam of your coffee at dawn,
        pale testimony to addiction, harmless,
        perhaps more so than others you want;
in one long-damaged knee
        whose cartilage resists your walk, and warns
        against a mock-tranquility;

in the bland and sweet obedience
>> of your dogs, which raises questions
>> that touch on your worthiness, competence;
in the warmth (to which you'll return)
>> of shelter, so easily canceled should your fuel
>> withhold its fire—a residue of the sun;
in fire, that has the power and glory
>> of "the things that have been made," as St. Paul says,
>> commanding faith, however airy;
in warmth and shelter and fire,
>> to which of course you will return,
>> for which you are whetting desire;
in desire, whose quenching is life
>> and death, as poets used to say—
>> by enjoinder and designation: husband, wife;
in this cheery fall of siskins
>> to an earth that you'd thought barren: in their number,
>> that may be somewhere counted, their busy-ness;
in their vanishing
>> —before you can count them yourself—
>> that sermonizes vanity;
in the far waw of a power saw
>> that binds on a softwood's sap, congealed:
>> the logger swears profanely, we are not healed;
in the warming recollection of your children,
>> for whose sake you pray as you can for death
>> to have no dominion, that you are forgiven.

The Floating Candles

—*for M.K.L., again*

You lit a firebrand:
old pine was best.
It lasted, the black
pitch fume cast odors
that, kindling a campfire
or such, today
can bring tears. You held
the torch to one dwarf
candle stub then another
and others till each
greased cup filled up
and the stiff wicks stood.
Ten minutes a candle,
but we were young
and minutes seemed long
as the whole vacation.
We chafed and quarreled.
The colors bled
like hues in jewels.
At last we carried
a tub of the things
down the path to the Swamp

Creek pond through seed-
heavy meadows where katydids
whined like wires
in mid-August air's
dense atmosphere.

An hour before bedtime.
Reluctant grown ups
would trail behind,
bearing downhill
the same dull patter
and cups brimful
of rye, which they balanced
with the same rapt care
that balanced our load.
The bullfrogs twanged
till you touched a wick
with the stick, still flaming,
then quieted. We heard them
plop in the shallows,
deferring to fire,
and heard in the muck
turtles coasting in flight.
The night brought on
a small breeze to clear
the day that all day
had oppressed us, to dry
the sweat that our purposeful
hour had made,
to spread the glims
like dreamboats of glory
in invisible current.
That slow tug drew
the glowing flotilla
south to the dam.

The bank brush—hung
with gemmy bugs—shone
and made great shadows
as the candles slipped by,

erasing the banal
fat stars from the surface.
This was, you could say,
an early glimpse
of a later aesthetic.
Nonsense. We know
it was cruder than that
and profounder, far.
It showed us the way
the splendid can flare
despite the flow
of the common. Now,
despite the persistence
of heat and quarrel,
the thickness of wives
and children and time,
such shinings on water
are fact. Or sublime.

In the Blind

—for Tommy White, my oldest friend

As in water face answers to face, the Proverb says,
so the mind of man reflects the man . . .
which must in my case mean the surface is roiled
as this one before me when it's lashed by furious beavers.
What a lot of time I spend in the blind,
splashing from thought to thought,
moving at random.
And how often I reach for you,
we shared so much, we rode all over God's acre
together, and always thought the same.
Now that we shoot toward fifty,

what does it all add up to?
Quick birds that breast the sun and rob my breath;
the revelation of internal pattern
in a fireplace log
at the moment my axe lays it open,
before I throw it on the heap
to dry, to be burned. Whiffs of memory.
Is the beautiful random enough?
Everything that is here and must go away.
(I wonder if you have time
for all this stuff.)

Sometimes late in November,
the river will suddenly turn austere, abstract,
as if its waves would cease their movement, stiffen.
Maybe you remember

how we used to argue over religion.
Especially in the fall,
it seems I still expend a lot of my life
waiting for something to light beside me and stay.
How often I'll be here,
the marsh alive around me
—something that riffles the slough, a rustle in weeds—

but the sky so empty only thought can fill it.
Except for the slow-motion stars. And except for Queen Moon:
just this morning, perfectly round,
she still was high, and my thought was of you
one time when you offered me a confession,
and it was hard,
for we thought of ourselves as rock-hard adolescents.

"Sometimes," you said, "I could cry
when I hear that Christmas carol,
'O Little Town of Bethlehem.'"

I laughed. I know exactly what you mean,
though we don't anymore have much in common
except this past that speaks to us in symbols
—the important part, at least—
and usually mutely.
It's that part about the deep and dreamless sleep,
am I right?
That, and the way the silent stars go by.
I think I knew even then what I feel now,
however hard of expression.
This morning, I say, the moon was full,

and there I was, half-asleep,
in my ignorance waiting for some wondrous declension,
the advent of . . . what?

There are moments in the blind
when I could simply lay back my head and bellow.
Do you remember those summer evenings
in your father's Rocket 88
when we'd fly back and forth like swallows
trapped in a building?
Here to there to there to here!
And yet we felt ourselves free,

the radio loud, loudly singing along.
Remember the Dells' old anthem?
"O, What a Night."
We didn't know where we were going,
but everything on the way was so perfectly lovely
—the silent little towns winking like planets,
the rolling frost-studded country—
moment to moment to moment,
what could it matter?
Over the undulant doo-wop, that falsetto.
Something also that hovered above us,

at least we thought so.
Some ever-available charm. I yet can see,
as if they were caught in a mirror,
our heads thrown back in song,
eyes to the sky,

improvising harmony, light like a symbol
of something up there, sure and answerable.
Possible, undivided, great.
As if we were not moving at all.
Streaming down on each kindred face,
a light like grace.

Pianissimo

Although I've claimed to know the language well,
So gentle is his call, so low—a vowel,
A breath—small wonder that its pain escapes me.

I've left behind my glasses: when he falls,
Beside a vineyard, in a field, downhill,
At first I lose him. Tiny in the poppies,

He seems a figure from some magic tale,
Flower stems the bars of his soft jail.
Can that sweet call have meant, *Signore, save me?*

Just now I might be anywhere at all,
A tourist only, from another world.
I might be hiking any other valley.

What he whispers next I can't quite tell,
Though once I claimed I knew this language well.
I think, though, every other word's *morire*.

Things seem far too still, as in some spell
Or dream in which one needs to run and fails.
I'm locked in gentle dusk in the Chianti,

The broom in bloom, whose magical sweet smell
Configures with some Angelus's bell.
At that, where might I run? I lift him gently,

Like a baby. On a ruined wall,
A lizard shows a pulse, redundant, small,
Like tickings of the watch I've left behind me,

On my holiday, with time to kill.
Only such slight fibrillations tell
He lives at all. 0 spell, 0 sweet *far niente:*

Lost to deed and word alike, I fall
Into your snares. This stillness overall
Will find his heart at last. My will betrays me.

An ox uphill lows gently from a stall.
The tiny man breathes softly still, *Signore,*
No longer, though, I think, to me at all.

Or is the word, I wonder, still *morire*?
I'm just a tourist here in the Chianti,
So much of this soft dialect escapes me.

The Return: Intensive Care

in mem. David Field

I felt for the button . . .
There's a circle of perpetual occultation
at the depressed pole,
within which stars never rise,
and at the elevated one, one of apparition
from which they never fall.
I used these facts
to figure the limits of my situation
—mine? or was it yours?—
as again I came back.

Where was I?
I thumbed the button for your floor.
It lit.
Suddenly, I thought,
everywhere there are circles,
as in some new weather or fashion:
the breasts both of a young farm girl
and, sadder, of a fat old orderly
riding up beside me;
the elevator's orbicular lamp-bulbs;
and, the color of linen,
each drop of snow the night before,
big and round as a saucer—
a night such as we persist in
calling a freak, though it isn't
anything more than the cycling back of things
too cursedly familiar.

Yes, though it was spring,
though it was April,
the moon had worn a great wet halo.

Signifying what?
Why look up
the facts on charts?
How often in history
has everything happened!
The nurse again wheeled away
your tray with its apple, untouched,
and two dark plums
that perfectly matched,
in color and conformation,
the raccoon rounds
through which your eyes peered,
brighter, still, than any planet.

O Jesus Jesus Jesus
inwardly I cried,
to me the word
recurring like any old habit.
Poor stately Jew, forgive the helplessness
that enforced my genteel outward mode
as you lay there,
my small-talk Yankee palaver
of mercilessness in Mother Nature—
buds in remission,
pathetic birds
spiraling up from the sheeted roads
as if, I surmised, nothing now remained
but vertical migration.

I dropped my eyes. All else, anything
that I might have been moved to say,

anything that might have reached to the heart
of what we may or may not be
here on earth
to do or serve, dismayed
and frightened me.
I couldn't speak
of anything beyond the trivial,
by horror of risk held back,
by horror of saying something
even more banal.

You were on morphine,
you who for the length of this evil illness
had never complained
but had made for yourself a figure
—*Look to the light,*
or, *Don't try to cling . . .*
Shy of prayer,
desperate with my own feckless
impulse to speech, at length I hung
as if in mid-air
as the dark outside
began again its round.
All so wretchedly dignified!

In the distilled absence of sound,
I recalled my *why why why why why*
at the death of my small terrier.
What a petty thing to remember!
And yet perhaps those yelps
when I was so young
were the only eloquence possible.
As was perhaps the gentle rejoinder
(she had seen more than I)

of my mother's mother:
Revelation helps.

There in the hospital,
lacking for words to tender,
I had recourse to fashion.
Forgive me, I nattered;
then left, once more pushing the button;
then lifted my eyes,
searching a sign of perpetuation.
Would it do any good to tell you that I cried?

There were stars, or there were none,
from wherever it was I stood.
There was, or there wasn't, a moon.

Road Agent

> *When the sun rises, they get them away*
> *and lie down in their dens. Man goes forth to his*
> *work and to his labor until the evening.*
>
> —Ps. 104

It doesn't seem so cursed in summer.
If a job could ever turn sweet, that's when.
There's just a little brush to tend.
Or I cuff the washboard flat with the grader.

You don't even have to swat the flies.
Diesel-smoke and noise will drive them.
The best is, I can look to the mountain.
The seat will raise a man that high.

The plow's high, too, but you can't look off.
Sun-up to sun-down, eyes on the road.
The mountain's still there when it goes cold.
But in winter you have to mind yourself.

Your help will quit you sure as Judas.
I clear the ice and snow on my own.
Everyone seems to go to den.
Kiss them good-bye when the weather freezes.

They call on the town or move to the city.
It's soft, but it isn't by Jesus my way.
I'm not like the state boys out on the highway.
I don't despise what isn't easy.

I'm what I was made, and nothing else.
I mean to earn my bread by sweat.
Foolish, the things that some expect.
God helps them that help themselves.

Some can't dream why I keep at it.
It's no matter what this one and that one say.
They vote me back on town meeting day.
But the new folks' notions and mine are different.

(The old-timers don't much like to talk.
I do it for them—I'm elected.
It comes with the work, and I guess it's expected.)
The newcomers squawk and I squawk back.

First thing to do, they say, is the schoolyard.
They have to get at the books, those kids!
(True, it's what my mother said.
The times would pass me by, she figured.)

But someone should bless the poor in school.
Everyone better not turn out bright.
They do, and these roads close down tonight.
They could own the world and lose their souls.

That's in a book, and makes some sense.
I graduated with less than I brought.
Of course I started going with Hat.
You couldn't call it a total loss.

We've kept on going, with six good children.
Say that for some that study college.
Say they got that out of all their knowledge.
Say they got it from education.

Road Agent

Last week I was working Sutter's Knoll.
I came on poor young Mrs. Grayson.
She had this little flimsy dress on.
You'd judge she was out for a summer stroll.

Her husband's diplomas would fill a trunk.
(Half-bare, she was, in a foot of snow!
I pretended a wing was loose on the plow.)
He's one of those jacket-and-necktie drunks.

Town Hall's the next that's got to be done.
The politicians insist on that.
They're damned important, you can bet.
I guess I oughtn't to run them down.

They hang on tougher than lots of others.
Take what few are left in The Grange.
It seems so quick, the way it's changed!
There aren't that many around to remember.

Things were different here one time.
The Grange is ready to fall on the ground.
Who cares nowadays in town?
I do it early, all the same.

Let them fire me: I've lived through worse.
It wasn't Happily-Ever-After.
It wasn't Everyone-Love-Your-Neighbor.
And the good Lord knows the money was scarce.

Then I plow the American Legion Post.
(There was always a battle or two somewhere.)
Schooling, politics and war.
Father, Son, and Holy Ghost.

I'm not even supposed to do the church.
That road is twisty, even in light.
I wait and fuss with it in the night.
Taxpayer money—they'd moan and bitch.

Dead last, this house of God out here.
But He says from the mountain, The last will be first.
In the end, He says, the first'll be last.
This is the one I fight to get clear.

The hardest one, in the cold of the year.

Over Brogno

> . . . *if from behind the stars the perilous archangel*
> *came down our thunderous heartbeats would kill us.*
>
> —Rilke

After the ten or twenty
        quiet minutes
                within the empty
church at San Giovanni,
                the lisping wavelets of the Como arm
                of the lake even less audible
                than the little implosions of dove-flight
                in the tower above like the shuffle
                of cards in a deck—

After my bourgeois
        reverie and rote prayers
                for the absent ones,
wife, children, friends,
                the lungs and torso at length light
                as wings as thought was transformed
                by consciousness of the cosmos below,
                the thronged dead, their buoyant
                deep dust

beneath soft stone
        on which I sat
                all weightless now in the pew—
the bells of noon
                had the *ploosh* sound of iron anchors
                cast over into water.

                        I stepped out onto the dazzled piazza,
                        near blind to the chic *ragazza*
                        who smiled a greeting

as she passed
            to the wharf's corner
            where she'd eat and read her glossy review.
Her womanhood weighted me too,
                        and thus I made my sudden decision
                        to turn, rise, go
                        south to the snowy mountain
                        along the ancient mule paths,
                        avoiding the heavy
trucks, clutched
            lovers, cars
                        so close I could almost touch them
on the wire-thin limestone
                        roads banked high with rock, where escape
                        seemed all but hopeless.
                        I wanted to rise above it all, withdraw
                        from millennia's mulched refuse
                        underneath me,

innocent as it was,
            innocent as the Virgin
                        whose icons at every
bridge across the *torrente*
                        were littered with candle, flower, coin—
                        earthy leavings and spillings
                        of quick and dead alike, moving
                        back and forth and back
                        along these tracks

like the bent
            and hoary *contadino*
                        of whom I asked directions,

> who courtly and gravely gestured:
>> "At every fork, choose a way that climbs,
>> if you must." To him there clung
>> sweet dung, dirt, dust,
>> as to others I passed, whom passing,
>> I commended to God,

> *Addio*. At which
>> they would bow in respect,
>>> it seemed, but seemed bemused,
> as if the expression I used
>> signaled not greeting but intention.
>> Did I think I was climbing *a Dio*?
>> Did they smile because it was odd to encounter
>> someone like me over Brogno?
>> Or at the superstition

That the higher powers
> are something one has
>> to seek in a higher order?
But they returned to their labors.
> Enough had passed on these mountain paths
> that another oddness could pass.
> Somewhere within my heart I thanked them,
> for only a troubled abstraction
> could have been my answer

if they had asked me
> where I was going.
>> And what was this humming, far past the final
boulder-built hovel?
> There on the summit, in the absence of wind,
> the tall tower, the unfleshed
> skull and bones on the chilling sign
> —*Pericolo di morte!*
> And something seen

or seemingly seen,
    an immanence, an aura.
        I thought beyond
to our time's angelic throngs:
        What deadly secrets? What secret soarings?
        What particles abroad?
        What specters of light that is more than light?
        Brogno far below,
        its inn and bar,

and I up there,
    and what radio waves winging by
        and bearing what lethal
abstraction from what capital,
        what lecture hall, what briefing room?
        Clamorous heartbeat, its clap
        within like thunder. Without, the Angel.
        I felt the heart must burst
        or draw me down

to cottage and shack,
    to human traffic,
        where souls move close to ground.

III. Wonder

For Faith

All had a look and meaning, she remembers.
The spirals of birds—adieu—in autumn's bluster.
Sun turning shadows from gray to black, and darker.
Notes on the brittle hymnal pages, signatures . . .
Clouds, swelled in the tawny highland pastures
till they looked like snow on sand.
Gales that boded fair or ugly weather,
and the northward lake's consequent moods and colors.
Or something indoors, like wood mites fretting the rafters.

The ancient organ's keys are chilly, tan,
but they warm and even brighten under her hand.
Crackle of August grasshoppers all through the land
so loud she feared that the timothy-stubble burned.
For prelude, something noble, *forte*, grand.
The tiny choir in her mirror,
sleep in their eyes. Can she stir them still? She can.
Outside, resplendent, scarlet in Sabbath sun,
a convertible-top Corvette: it's hers, who ran

with her lucent, blood-bay mare beside her father,
riding astride in the piquant vacations of Easter:
shine of mane in the breezes; gull-squawks; lather;
turf, puddle, saddle-soap, evergreen, leather;
new grass rolling in waves to mimic the water's.
Or the naked cardinal plant,
Oriental in hailstone-pearled northeasters.
Or a chirr in the pantry: the laboring separator.
And her voice, so achingly clear, that makes these over. . . .

Season after season, arriving, turned:
Summer's giant evenings, late to begin
and coming like fog or scent so stealthily on,
as playful, she hid with her restive dogs in the barn.
At *c* above staff, there's one odd pipe that groans.
She has been the familiar
of this organ a long long time: the stop that pretends
it is *vox humana*, the autonomous *f* that sounds
if you hold the leftmost pedal too far down,

or mutes itself in the tonic chord for *d*-minor.
So much of this depends upon the weather.
The muteness, as well, and the pallor of her father,
sprawled in mud next to a calf he'd delivered.
Staring at whitecaps through kitchen windows, Mother
wheezed in rhythm, her hands dropped listless beside her.
How throaty, the sports car's motor:
it's not, however, something she'll consider,
leaving it all behind. She raises a finger,

hoping Janette of the quavery alto will note her,
will alter a flatness; or maybe she as director
will take her part and sing it louder and drown her.
And still Janette will love her. That's the wonder.
So I think—quiet as a mime in my corner—
dreaming I understand.
Now, as the anthem follows, she starts all over.
If I'm wrong, still something rich and grand must move her
and make that light a fool could see above her.

Ghost Pain

—in mem. Jim Kilgo

Murmured conversation like simmering water.
Happy looking clothes.
We're easy to mock, and aren't we hypocrites, you ask?
Nowhere does faith claim we're not.
Hypocrisy comes with the territory:
being human. Roof and rafters and steeple snap.

It's minus ten degrees out there,
for the love of Christ,
and it seems above all so safe inside,
safer even than home.
It seems home.
We've lit the half-blighted spruce by the road,

chanted our way through a tone-deaf carol,
repaired to our coffee and small talk.
Brian just wheeled in Joan.
We wish them all the cheer that humans can,
inquire how the leg is,
now that it's gone.

Is there ghost pain?
Brave Joan and Brian kindle like matches.
It's their anniversary, and they're proud
of their grown daughter, who lately recited a poem,
a wonderful awful poem to a lost mother.
She'd found it on the Internet, she crowed

in her joy, a brand new adventure.
She used it in tribute to her grandma, Joan's mother.
The hour was all about tribute, memory, loss:
we'd each brought a bulb for the tree;
we screwed them into waiting sockets on boughs,
light for parents, grandparents, uncles, aunts,

lost children and friends. Ghost pain.
Then we went in a crowd to the vestry,
Mary among us,
happy she could make her way in her walker
after the doctors put her knee back together.
Red stayed home with Agnes,

too sick with the chemo to come.
We'd prayed for them,
for Willie who died wife- and childless,
for others, many others, saints and strangers.
We're proud of our youngest daughter,
who performed "One Little Candle" at the start of the service.

She sings like an angel, but it's the poise that stuns
her mother and me,
but why should it make us cry?
A dear friend down south has gone;
his church's prayer chain couldn't hold him.
Not this time. People die.

The stars outdoors are sharp as razors,
and Orion the Hunter huge and bold above the river—
as if he could send an arrow flying right through us here.
All manner of things fly through the No-Fly Zone
elsewhere, the homeless huddle under cardboard,
all the brutal rest, and no, since you inquire,

we can't account for it. It's Pearl Harbor Day,
hours of light down to nine, to fewer.
If God be for me, whom then shall I fear?
Easy enough to say, the mockers might say, from in here.
I might be out there among them
were the world not served,

we have to believe, in there being
one more safe tiny place amid the great unsafe.
The girl sang well, enough to bring tears.
A small voice got big, rose over the pain.
And thus did Mary trudge in,
and Joan roll in on her chair,

and Red and Agnes and Willie figure thus in our prayers,
and the only miracle for this lonely minute:
we were inside,
even those who weren't, who aren't, who can't be.
And the wind that blows no good—
it's outside.

And the cookies are good, and the coffee.
By God aren't they good?

—December 7, 2002

Hole

"I'll be quick," he says, and he is.
To speak to our group you're required to qualify
so he begins: "We found the bottom of stupid and dug us a hole."

He says at the end he was runnin on empty.
He says even in the joint they didn't have no trouble gettin product
and once when they couldn't, why, a bunch of them shot up whatever,
fools

that they all was—even lighter fluid, skim off of boiled mayonnaise.
And then some died, or started floppin around "like chickens
after you axe them." (He was raised a farm kid,

never mind the crude blue stupid tattoos).
Just like he was sayin,
the bottom of stupid. The bottom: that was it,

and the hole we dug below it. The hole we all dug.
"They did that partly because they loved the spike.
It's crazy: they loved the drug first, true,

but also the spike." There is stupid and stupid
of course, he says, because in some ways they wasn't stupid.
Like they learnt how you could go to the rec room and when the screw

was noddin or readin or talkin to someone else
you yanked out a wire from the beat-ass piano.
Now if you could get a Walkman motor and a bottle cap,

you could put the motor in the cap and fill the cap with ink
and take that plastic tube from a ballpoint
and run the wire through it down in the ink. That was that,

your tattoo kit: start the motor, the wire's your needle, slicker'n shit.
He has *Truth* on his left forearm for some reason.
He has *1%* on his right.

He says *Charlene*'s on a buttock, but of course he doesn't show us.
He says he don't know what God is and truth is,
he don't care: somehow or another he's right

here with us, "And meantime a lot of them's dead or crazy or still in stir—
so why me? Why any of us?" He thanks God.
He remembers how he read about the wise man's knowledge

turnin out to be foolish. Read it in solitary (for the tattoos). In the hole.
And the fool's foolishness the other way around.
He was both a wise-ass and a fool—no high school, let alone college—

so if he has any wisdom he's here to prove a fool can get it.
There's a lot of appreciative laughing, but some of us
feel more than a little uncomfortable with the God stuff so we stay silent.

Some of us don't really want him to read
what he reads, which is Psalm 28, including the part that says
O Lord my rock be not silent to me lest if thou be silent

I become like those who go down in the pit.
He's a Bible nut someone whispers.
But then again we are all of us alive.

A lot of people aren't. That mayonnaise stunt. The lighter fluid.
The time when one of us drove through the bridge
across the river and we hung till we got saved.

The time one of us came to in our bathroom
with the toilet seat all bashed to bits
in the mess of puke on the floor and we stood up and didn't know
ourselves

and fell again and stood up again
and the blood was like a brown mask on our face in the mirror.
We didn't know our own face but we didn't die.

Down in the pit. Down in the bottom of stupid.
"Someone, I don't know what it would be . . . or something,"
he claims—"Something could hear me cry."

—*Windsor State Prison, 2002*

At a Solemn Musick

For the Connecticut Valley Youth Choir

i. *After looking into my grandmother's hymnal*

Closing the little book with care—so brittle,
Dated Christmas 1899—
I stood in the sleeping house, then stole outside

To where last evening's first flake settled
On my sleeve and for the scantest moment shone,
Then vanished. A moment only, in which I might

Have dreamed up other moments, each so gone
So quickly. So I did, but also dreamed
Myself ahead to now. I dreamed in joy

Of such sweet airs as now will settle on
Me and this company. The keyboard's strains.
The flake-white church. Your keen director's poise.

The yellowed pages turn. What's here will dim
And crumble, blurring column on column on column.
And yet for the moment we have our broken haven.

I won't hear words of one forgotten hymn
From my father's mother's surviving sacred volume:
Praise Him, o ye Heaven of Heavens.

Nor will I hear *The children answering.*
Still, *let their guileless song re-echo,*
And their heart its praises bring.

We elders know too well how darkness gathers
And swallows down the year, and how the darkness
In days to come will turn to even darker.

Tonight, however, perhaps we may remember
How child- and tuneful glories will outlive us,
And how in them some thing lives on forever.

ii. *Children singing*

It's the time of year when listening to a child
  Becomes a way to pray.
Praise newborn God, we think, all *mercy mild*,
  And may He gain our day.

Before us here a choir of heavenish voices,
  Children's voices, say,
As the anthem demands, *Our weary world rejoices*.
  Just what are we to pray?

That we *become*—as writings prophesy—
  As little children? That we *hark*—
Hearing the carol—as *herald angels sing?* They'll fly
  Breakneck from innocence to dark-

Tinged wonder, Incarnation flown to Passion.
  But singing children—They,
Like Bethlehem's Infant, salve such apprehension.
  From the manger *where He lay*,

The center of a universe now blessed,
A childlight charging every note and rest.

Wonder: Red Beans and Ricely

for Christopher Matthews

He blew the famous opening figure of "West End Blues"
and then . . . A long pause. A long long pin-drop pause.
This sounded like nothing the four of us had been hearing out here
at the Famous Sunnybrook Ballroom in East Jesus, PA,
which was in fact a moth-eaten tent to which in summer
the post-war big bands, then fading into the fifties—
the likes of the Elgars or Les Brown and His Band of Renown—
would arrive to coax the newly middle-aged and their elders
into nostalgia and dance. My cousin, our pretty steadies
and I were younger, cocksure, full of contraband beer,
but the moment I speak of knocked even us in the know-it-all chops.

I suddenly dreamed I could see through the tent's canvas top
clear up to stars that stopped their fool blinking and planets that stood
stock-still over cows and great-eyed deer in the moonlight
and ducks ablaze on their ponds because everything in God's world
understood this was nothing like anything they'd known before.
It's still a fantasy, that sorry tent a lantern,
transparent as glass, through which I beheld the landscape around it
as though it showed in some Low Country more-than-masterpiece
while no one danced. The crassest fat-necked burgher in the crowd
sat rapt, as did his missus, the moment being that strong.
It lingered strong, beginning to end, through the blues that followed.

Then Velma Middleton got up to jive and bellow.
She broke the charm, her scintillant dress like a tent itself,
and people resumed the lindy and foxtrot as she and he
traded the always-good-for-laughs double meanings

of "Big Butter and Egg Man," "That's My Desire,"
and so on. And so we four, or rather we two boys,
resumed our drinking and boasting until the band took its break.
Full enough by now of the Bud and some of the rum
that the cousin had brought—which would take him in too sadly short a time
away to another shore forever—I stood and pledged:
I'll get his autograph. It made no sense at all.

I staggered to and through the canvas's backstage hole,
the mocking jibes of cousin and sweethearts dying behind me,
and beheld a row of semi- trucks: his equipage.
There were two doors as to a house in each, and a little set
of metal steps underneath. Without a hitch, I climbed
one stair of the bunch. It made no sense except it did.
I *knew*. . . . Something had burned into my reeling brain
when that opening solo started, and the man would have to be
just there where he was when I knocked on one of the several doors
inside the trailer, and the growl was Fate: it didn't surprise me:
Come in, he said. How could he? How could he not? I came.

It was meant to be, and still I stammered with puzzlement, shame.
I'd had a vision, yes, and yet to have the vision
there before me. . . . Wonder! Great Armstrong at a desk
in an undershirt, suspenders flapping, his face near blinding,
sweat-beads charged by the gimcrack rack of fluorescent lights
so that he seemed to wear an aura—it was all
one supple motion, the way he reached into a drawer,
drew out a jug of Johnny Walker, sucked it down
to the label, squared before him a sheet of paper, ready
for me, it seemed, flourished a fountain pen and wrote:
Red Beans and Ricely Yours at Sunny Brook Ballroom . Pops.

Back at the table they judged it was real enough by the looks.
"I just walked in and got it," I bragged, as if a miracle
hadn't transpired, as great as any I'd ever know.

I bragged as if my part in it all were important somehow,
and God hadn't just looked down and said, *Well okay—him.*
And what remains from then? Not the paper, long since lost,
nor the lovely, silken girls, Sally and Barbara,
nor the cousin, as I've said, who crossed the foulest river,
nor that brash, that truly and stunningly blessèd younger I,
nor the heaven-struck beasts and the trees and the moon and the sky.

Just a handful of opening notes from a horn which are there forever.

Barnet Hill Brook

Here's what to read in mud by the brook after last night's storm,
Which inscribed itself on sky as light, now here, now gone—

And matchless. I kneel in the mud, by scrimshaw of rodents, by twinned
Neat stabs of weasel. I won't speak of those flashes. Here by my hand,

The lissome trail of a worm that lies nearby under brush,
Carnal pink tail showing out. Gnats have thronged my face.

I choose not to fend them off. Except for my chest in its slight
Lifting and sinking, the place's stillness feels complete.

Its fullness too: in the pool above the dead-grass dam,
The water striders are water striders up and down:

They stand on themselves, feet balanced on feet in mirroring water.
How many grains of sand in the world? So one of my daughters

Wanted to know in her little girlhood. "Trillions," I said.
"I love you," she answered back. "I love you more than that."

Lord knows I'm not a man who deserves to be so blessed.
I choose to believe that there's grace, that the splendid universe

Lies not in my sight but subsumes my seeing, my small drab witness.
Tonight my eye may look on cavalcades of brightness,

Of star and planet. Or cloud again. And when I consider,
O, what is man, That thou art mindful of him, it's proper

For me to have knelt, if only by habit. Pine needles let go,
And drop, and sink to this rillet's bright-white bottomstones.

To tally them up would take me a lifetime. And more would keep coming.
A lifetime at least. And more would keep coming, please God, keep
coming.

Dispute with Thomas Hardy

> *The smile on your mouth was the deadest thing*
> *Alive enough to have strength to die.*
>
> —"Neutral Tones"

It won't last long, this snow that sheathes
                      the dooryard pine in April and lays
its pale doomed cover on the slope behind.
                      Crocuses, just tall enough,
are poking their small pink noses through.
                      It's clear they're alive enough to live
though April's gale is artillery-loud.
                      What's left of ice around the pond
in town looks rough as predators' teeth.
                      Somewhere a fisher rips open a mouse.

There's much I too may try to cover,
                      which is why perhaps I feel strange gladness
to watch the omni-inclusive white
                      subsume the neutral tones that pushed
our brilliant poet to ponder death
                      and love's deception, its cruelty.
We've been together, my love and I,
                      near three decades, which have scudded by
like these sideways flakes. My mortal wife. . . .
                      There *can* come pangs. But freshets have started

to wander the brush and leave their signs.
                      Soon we'll find the trillium,
the painted kind, in the hidden place,

        which I discovered ten springs ago
and which since then I've kept a secret
       from all but her—from even our children;
and the valley's white-faced Herefords
        dropped new calves while winter endured.
Mud and blood yet cling to the cows
       but the calves shine clean as a colorful dream.

What dream would be mine? That life go on,
      that all humanity go on.
No more than dream, of course, I know,
       the planet heating up, the cretin
politicians rattling swords,
       as if, by counter-logic, war
transmuted the earth into something saintly.
       The harder facts conspire against me.
Yet to know as much is to make me cling
       the harder to gifts apparently given

without my having at all to deserve them:
      flowers, animals, glinting trees,
and a disposition that moves me here
       to disputation with my great better,
in spite of all my darker doubt.
       Inkling of something soon to come down
like rain upon mown grass, as showers
       that water the earth. Some Lordly power,
or at least new weather. Or the smile on the mouth
       of that lover-wife, which blinds like snow.

Or the road agent waving from his bright-red plow
       as it smoothes the drifted back lanes over.

Transport

—Church of St. Francis, Prague, July 2003

After the tourist's two blue insomniac nights,
patrols of all that had been lost, botched, or sweet
but severed, during the Albinoni he went off,
up, away, so that if, say, the sudden recall
of his late mother in grainy portrait in her yearbook,
over the captions: "brightest," and—in the quaint patois
of the gentry during their Depression—"most attractive,"
and the despair she may have felt as children and alcohol
supervened: if any such feckless maundering
occurred to him. . . . Well, off, up and away went she
as well, borne heavenward on the andante's strains.
Two trumpets. One great organ. Peace might well lie at hand.
Peace was at hand. During Martini's toccata in C,

a vision of his tall naked wife, under a tall naked sun,
produced in him in the church a subtle stirring, even
a mild tumescence, which he would otherwise have described
as out of order, were it not that this newer order arched
so beyond any scheme he'd normally posit that within it all things
were possible, as they are, it is said, with God, Who
during the Manfredini revealed Himself to our tourist
in what he construed as His human form, His prison garb
stained and rent, His savaged body hefted by men
and women—their countenances looking more angry than mournful—
from a loud place like that bar on the corner of Thakurova
and Evropska, which he had walked by that evening on his way
to transport: the Metro, which carried him into this old quarter

in a car along with that beauteous, amorous young Czech couple
with their red-tipped white staffs and whited eyes,
then spilled him out to rump steak with garlic, alone, and then
to the 9 p.m. concert, alone. During the *Ave Maria*
of Schubert, he saw a joy he hadn't seen in the tears
of St. Peter as rendered face-forth by an artist, Swiss of all things,
unknown to him till that forenoon in the Castle gallery.
The wailing weanling calves of his childhood now placidly grazed.
The famous small songbirds lit on the outstretched arms of Francis.
Peter's tears had appeared only woeful this morning. The hour of music

concluded, the tourist walked, though it felt still like soaring,
his cobblestone-wearied heels devoid of any pain,
back into this world, broken and joyous and praying,

"Never to be the same." Never perhaps again.

Sober

So these were the Andes, and these the fabled *chollos*,
ponies strong enough to bear his flesh
and weight accrued
        —failed suicide, guilt and tears—
ten thousand feet to that world-commanding prospect.
The guide reported that one might with luck behold
a condor. A pair had nested here for years.

The horses surefooted shale that would scare a man
as he walked, the clouds hung mountain-vast, he hoped
the rain would wait:
        he imagined on his own
that his self, which counted so little among those grand
immensities, or anywhere, might wash
downhill to the crashing *rio*, on which his bones

would ride to the cold Pacific, dissolve within it,
as he once believed they were meant by fate to do.
Yet here he sat
        a noble horse. He was well.
Sweet wind conspired with the scents of lather, leather.
Years before, rock-bottomed, he'd never have dreamed a condor,
and still he all but feared a welcoming world.

The guide called out, *Serà allà!* The bird
would be up there. He pointed at crags
as bleak and boding
        as childhood terror. Gray.

The bird was not *allà*, would not be found
that day, and it came to him clear again that wonder
lay in the thought of God, which made him say,

O I have seen that soaring after all,
because he'd known what it can be to be
poised at an edge
         more deadly than any he climbed
just then. He felt as if he'd turned much lighter
than a lump of man like him had a right to turn.
Into his mind—or out of some greater mind—

the wide-flung wings came gliding, gold as sun.

IV. Six Sundays Toward a Seventh

—for the Reverend Malcolm Grobe

1
Do not trust in these deceptive words:

*This is the temple if the Lord,
The temple of the Lord. . . .*
First Lenten Sunday, and the Jeremiad

Reduces us to heretics,
Quite properly: the temple draws us inward
Yet again. "Québec Express"

—The wind along our glacial reach of river—
Penetrates through nail holes, sockets.
The fellowship, however, gathers.

Till service starts, we throw clichés at winter,
Chatting to unlock it,
Warm ourselves. The litany assures,

Its scope so narrow:
Oh yes, we say and pray, they'll all be here:
Jonquils; jobs; the chanting thrush; the sparrow. . . .

Blooms and babies, issues of the town.
How spring will nap the lawns.
Someone's good news to celebrate—

Remission. Calm. Some novel revenue
To keep the school afloat:
"Revenue," says Blaise: "The coming back."

It's not such puns nor platitudes that soothe
But how they do come back.
Not peace, we're warned. A sword.

Not, thus, to trust in children, flowers, birds?
Nor mist all raiment-soft on open water?
And not these words, nor pungency of lumber

That fell, before last fall, before the blade?
It isn't them we trust in any case
But their return, as sure as ours.

The season's myth declines to death,
And yet again, again, we park our cars
And move inside to speak our faith.

—JEREMIAH 7:4;
—MATTHEW 10:34

2

February—winter! lightning! thunder!

Blotched with passion, his girlish fingers
Clenched the wood on the back of the bench before him:
Flood made us late. We straggled in and saw him.

Stranger than Sunday's storm, this praying stranger
Who, when at last he straightened, turned to observe us,
It grew more rude than odd, his manner:

Jane, who bakes for Communion Service,
He reckoned over-dressed. He looked askance.
But he wrinkled his nose as well at the threadbare suit

Of Harley, everyone's friend, and his callused hands.
He scowled at Vernon the deacon, storekeeper, farmer,
Huge in gumboots—feisty, hirsute,

With a voice to front this freakish thunder.
Lightning galloped, insistent; untimely, rain
Smote the clerestory's stained memorial panes

For Ed, our late and moderate moderator.
God love us, a person might think, if this were The Christ,
Returned as it says He means to return.

The hymn begun, the voice of the guest
Had doubtless heft. (It soared in fact over Vernon's.)
Ended, polite, we asked him to make himself known.

He named no name. He said, instead: "I present you
The text of the morning: *Even the dust of your town
That clings to our feet we wipe off against you....*"

And *"I saw Satan fall like lightning
From heaven."* The wanderer rose with that, departed.
 "And we let the bastard preach, by God Almighty!"

So Vemon swears, as we talk on Monday about it,
Though surely he knows that ours is a common anger.
In fury, he flings his goods onto shelves:

He can't think surely that I will differ
In wrath at such an intruder—troublemaker!—
On us who love our neighbors, as much as ourselves.

—LUKE: 10–11; 10:17; 10:28

3

**In cold what we see are the
parson's wraithy breaths:**

*There are some standing here who will not taste death
Before they see His kingdom come with power.
. . . Jesus took with him Peter*

And James and John and led them up a mountain
—Where is the heat?—*and he was transfigured before them.*
I think of John my brother,

Distorting Scripture. We all should huddle together.
The frozen organ flats as a spirit might do.
I mumble: "I took with me two . . . ,"

Blaspheming. One was John, and Blaise the other.
We three crossed a mountain and down to a river.
In that photograph of Montana:

Around my John, transforming him, an aura.
The light is low, it's near the fall, it's evening.
Upstream he stands, feasting

On trout from an iron skillet, head and all.
That inchoate pattern on the scarp's bronze wall—
A handful of geese inscribing

Its *mene, mene, tekel* and *parsin*. Departing.
So many, the things of this world. I took up the camera.
The river boiled and stammered.

In cold what we see are the parson's wraithy breaths:

We heard coyotes at gossip, and bugling elk.
And there was something else that Blaise and I felt
More than we saw, as John,

With his fish and some wine, profane in the dying sun,
Feasted and drank and gloried in gold and silver,
Standing there upriver.

World: bronze, iron, wood, stone.
Blaise, and I, and all of these, and John,
And the heat of the breath that was coming,

As we shivered together there, and a greater something.
A bear coughed, sudden and near, unseen overhead.
And we shivered, standing there, with awe, undead.

—MARK, 9:1, 2;
—DANIEL, 5:25–28

4

Locked though we were in our own sick, aching flesh,

All night we tended our newborn as she squalled.
My eyes open hot. The whited chains of drool
Fasten her milk-blistered pout to my wife's left breast.

I must depart them, the slumbering woman and daughter,
Bound—or is it released?—in consciouslessness.
I make my hobbled, pedestrian rounds to the others:

Each child, however the mean dark's trials were protracted,
Is set in peace in the body now, it appears.
I could if I would fix all in a picture, and call it

Free and Serene. I teeter in front of a chair,
Inclined as I am at once to surrender and fight,
Blessing and cursing lame joints and labored breath.

In a cupboard, caffeine—a drug precisely right
Or wrong. My thick-boned hand is a quake on the shelf.
Inside, outside, upward, downward, death.

A redpoll, one of the daily many misguided,
Has struck a pane. The twitch of its remnant claws:
Sad as a spastic's dancing. There beside it,

A blood-mustachio'd cat now contemplates,
Lion-lazy and -lordly, tenantless space.
What can it see in such air, as dim as dungeons'?

False spring's ice has flayed our Flowering Crab.
Daniel asserts: *He rescues and delivers.*
So, at the service this morning, it will be read;

Well, let them read, how his God works signs and wonders,
On heaven and earth. At home I rest unassured,
And side with that side of Paul the Letter-Writer,

Late out of prison, which claims he would depart,
Claims he would be with Christ, for that is far better. . . .
Shut in self-pity, I'd disregard how he added,

To be in the flesh is more needful on your account;
Or how Jesus chided a lame one, *Take up your pallet,*
Breaking the Sabbath, commending our worldly rounds.

—DANIEL, 6:27;
—PHILIPPIANS, 1:23, 24

5

Guy and Robert do it the older way:

Single pails, draft horse and sleigh.
No garish plastic tubing. No four-wheel drive.
Fifth Lenten Sabbath—a sugaring day.

By your endurance you will gain your lives.
Last night's chill moon, blue stars and blasts of aurora
Seemed wonders in darkness, powers.

But we're not yet there. The morning's fair.
Robert and Guy, with Joli, their great blond gelding,
Slave in the damp corned snow.

Or say they endure.
"Slave"—that shouldn't be the word,
Since lo, these generations ago,

Uprose the maple trade against brute harvests
of cane by blacks
on steaming southern plantations.

How might so white a March be further from that?
(Oh yes, there's the steam,
In plumes above the infernal sugar shack,

And shimmering over the frames of the men and Joli.)
No one should live like a beast. . . .
A new dawn's breaking, and we're enjoined to be ready,

Lest that day come upon you suddenly.
I think of the trees,
Of acid winging in on rain from the west,

Coming in a cloud. Can it be a sign?
The maples persist in sweetness,
And Guy and Robert in archaic business,

And there will be signs in stars and sun and moon.
St. Paul ponders the doom of those
With minds set on earthly things,

And our pastor recites the warnings of Luke 21.
What is the part of these laborers in snow?
The Day may be coming soon, but until then . . .

—LUKE 21:25
—PHILIPPIANS 3: 19

6
The shroud of white is leaching from

The village common. The ragged humble return
To aim their Geiger counters over mud.
What has frost thrown up?

Keys to no door, bent coins, drained cans
And foil—aluminum:
Bright as angels, devoid of value,

History-less. Still Jim and Mickey wave.
Their women smoke in a relic GMC. . . .
At church now Harley reads

The proper Scripture, smoothing out the page:
You'll always have them with you,
The poor, deluded Mickeys, Jims,

The whey-faced wives . . . who might be better off,
I've thought, if they could sit among us here.
Alone in awkward prayer

—In which I name whatever haunts me Love—
Can I invite them in:
The spirit is willing, but the flesh is weak.

The Palms of welcome lie on the spotless altar,
Limp. *Ride On, Ride On, In Majesty;*
Let this cup pass from me—

In mind, the song and Gospel swim together
As silly clicks and beeps
Outside suggest some other find,

Unblessed. Three times I've passed these common seekers:
Once, as I rode down to buy the *Times*,
Again on my way home,

And last arriving here, a week from Easter—
Passed them as if blind
In study of corrupted masks of snow.

I will strike the shepherd, the sheep will be scattered.
So was it prophesied.
And as he spoke the cock began to crow.

—MATTHEW 26

7

**Still dark when we file like
children out on the turf,**

Yet our hymn is For the Beauty of the Earth.
Irony scourges. Is that how grown-ups atone?
The apostate, Jack, is back with us. It's cancer.

We've gathered, we few others, by the river
For other reasons, whatever. Where's the sun?
Sunrise Service. Easter. Ice on the waters.

In the flow, among black limbs, a jug bobs past us,
Empty, thrown perhaps by a drunken angler
Who waited through last fall but never caught him,

The fish he'd prayed for, childlike—unseeable, awesome.
We here know life is hard but for some promise.
We murmur *For the Love which from our birth. . . .*

Debris, relentless, eddies down from north.
I imagine the fisherman, grown more doubtful than Thomas:
One dusk he flung away the jug, the dream.

Is that a Christmas present, still in its carton?
Over and around us lies, we sing.
We have mouthed the store-bought dough, the bitter wine.

They are real enough, the wounds we've seen.
Last Wednesday, shocked, we buried redoubtable Vernon.
We'd all feel different, maybe, in different weather.

It would seem somehow less willed, this banding together.
We have left undone the things we ought to have done,
And the other way round. Jane's at the clinic. Neurosis.

Harley's halt again. Accursed phlebitis.
Flotsam—fragmented story—drifts and spins.
What was it that the adulterous woman said?

A man who told me all I ever did.
The pastor opened by reading about her from John.
Lazarus too. And the blind man's pool at Siloam.

As a fish-eye sun slides open over the mountain,
Our children strain to break from us and play.
We end with This our hymn of grateful praise.

—JOHN 4:29; John 20:25; John 11; John 9

www.ingramcontent.com/pod-product-compliance
Lightning Source LLC
Chambersburg PA
CBHW022117090426
42743CB00008B/886